A Picture Book of

BABY ANIMALS

Written by Grace Mabie
Illustrated by Roseanna Pistolesi

Troll Associates

Library of Congress Cataloging-in-Publication Data

Mabie, Grace, (date)
 A picture book of baby animals / written by Grace Mabie; illustrated by
Roseanna Pistolesi.
     p.   cm.
   Summary: Introduces a dozen baby animals, including the wolf's
cub, the penguin's chick, and the cat's kitten.
   ISBN 0-8167-2468-7 (lib. bdg.)   ISBN 0-8167-2469-5 (pbk.)
   1. Animals—Infancy—Juvenile literature.   [1. Animals—Infancy.]
I. Pistolesi, Roseanna, ill.   II. Title.
QL763.M25   1992
599'.039—dc20   92-26264

CAT

This mother cat is cuddling her 4 new *kittens*. Kittens feel safe and warm when they lie next to their mother. She washes them, feeds them, and takes good care of them. A kitten cannot hear or see for about 2 weeks after it is born. By the time it is about 8 weeks old, the kitten can take care of itself and is ready to leave its mother.

Kittens are very playful. Playing helps them learn how to get along with other cats. It also teaches them how to hunt.

BEAR

A bear usually has 2 *cubs* at a time. Cubs are born during the winter, while the mother is resting in a warm, safe *den*. By the time spring comes, the young bears have grown a lot and are ready to go outside.

Cubs stay with their mother for a year or two. She teaches them how to find food. When the bears are old enough, they leave their mother and go off on their own. In a few years, the young bears will start their own families.

ELEPHANT

Elephants are the largest animals living on land. Even baby elephants are big! A *calf* weighs about 250–350 pounds (113–145 kilograms) when it is born, and is about 3 feet (1 meter) tall.

Elephants can live for 60 years or more. An elephant isn't grown up until it is about 10 years old. Until then, the calf stays with its mother. They live with other elephant families in large groups called *herds.*

CONDOR

A condor is a type of bird called a *vulture*. Vultures feed on animals that are already dead. A female condor usually lays 1 egg every other year, although sometimes she will lay 2. When the *chick* hatches, it is covered with soft feathers called *down*. Its mother and father have to bring food to it. In a few weeks, the chick will grow feathers and learn how to fly.

DOG

This *puppy* looks a lot like its mother! Many baby animals grow very fast. In just a few months, they look like small adults.

Puppies take 8 months to 2 years to grow up. Large dogs take longer than small dogs. During this time, a puppy's body changes very much. It is important that the puppy eats the right kind of food so it will grow up to be strong and healthy.

Most puppies are very curious and smart. They like to learn tricks and can be trained to help people in many ways.

MOUNTAIN GORILLA

These gentle animals live in the mountains of central Africa. They wander in groups of 2 to 30, looking for plants to eat. At night they sleep in nests on the ground or up in trees.

Female gorillas have one baby at a time. A gorilla only weighs 3–5 pounds (1.4–2.3 kilograms) when it is born. At first, its mother carries the baby in her arms as she searches for food. In a few months, the gorilla is strong enough to ride on its mother's back or walk along beside her.

OPOSSUM

Opossums are part of a special group of animals called *marsupials*. When opossums are born, they are very tiny and completely helpless. The babies crawl into a pouch on their mother's stomach. They stay there for about 2½ months, growing bigger and stronger. When they come out of the pouch, the mother carries the young opossums around on her back.

WOLF

Wolves live in large family groups called *packs*. All the wolves in the pack help take care of the *cubs*. For the first few months, the cubs depend on the adults to find food for them. But after about 6 months, the cubs and the adults begin to hunt together.

Wolves look a lot like dogs. That is because both wolves and dogs are part of the same family. But while dogs make good pets, wolves are too wild to live with people.

HORSE

A *foal* can stand up and walk soon after it is born. At first it wobbles on its long legs, but soon it will be able to gallop. A foal usually stays close to its mother. She nurses the foal, licks its coat to keep it clean, and takes care of it until the young horse is about 6 months old.

A male horse is called a *colt* until it is 4 years old. A young female is called a *filly*. Both colts and fillies have to be specially trained before people can ride them.

CHICKEN

There are many different kinds of chickens. But, like all birds, their babies hatch from eggs. A *chick* uses its sharp beak to break through the eggshell. Chicks can walk and find food as soon as they are born.

Chicks have a lot of trouble staying warm, especially at night when the temperature goes down. They snuggle close to their mother to share her body heat.

PENGUIN

There are many different kinds of penguins. These are called *chinstrap penguins* because of the dark line on their heads. Chinstrap penguins usually lay 2 eggs at a time. The *chicks* don't have all their feathers at first, so they cannot swim in the icy water. Their parents bring them tiny plants and animals to eat.

KANGAROO

   Kangaroos are marsupials. When it is born, a *joey* is blind, and very tiny. But its front legs are very strong. It uses them to pull itself through its mother's fur and into a pouch on her stomach. The joey stays in the pouch for about 6 months. As it gets older, the young kangaroo will come out of the pouch for short periods of time, but it stays close to its mother. When it is about 8 months old, the joey leaves the pouch for good.

Canada Goose

INDEX